heat

Bob Graham

Blackie

Jenny is in the garden.
It is much too hot to work.

Patch is Jenny's dog. It is too hot for Patch.
He is panting. Look at his tongue.

3

It's a bit too hot for Jenny too.

Patch has found a cool place
under a tree.

5

The leaves of the tree are like a
big green umbrella,
hiding Patch from the sun.

6

Jenny's feet feel hot and sticky.

What can Jenny do to cool her feet?

Jenny splashes cold water on her feet.
When they feel cool she ...

. . . sprays cold water on the rest of her.
Now Jenny feels lovely and cool.

Her droopy flowers may soon feel better too.

11

Jenny makes some puddles.
They will soon dry up in the heat.

Patch is cool enough.
He doesn't want to be
sprayed with cold water.

13

He hides in another cool, shady place.

So Jenny turns off the water.

When the sun goes down
it will be much cooler.